AUTHOR

Sharlyn Lauby
Sharlyn Lauby is an author, speaker, and consultant. She is best known for her work on HR Bartender, a site focused on workplace issues. Lauby is the author of *Manager Onboarding: 5 Steps for Setting New Leaders Up for Success* and *The Recruiter's Handbook: A Complete Guide for Sourcing, Selecting, and Engaging the Best Talent.*

Content Manager, Instructional Design
Eliza Blanchard, APTD

Editor, *TD at Work*
Patty Gaul

Managing Editor
Joy Metcalf

Graphic Designer
Shirley E.M. Raybuck

Managers play an important role in any organization. According to Gallup, they account for 70 percent of the variance in employee engagement—meaning good managers can have a positive effect on engagement, and poor managers … well, you get the point. Employee engagement has a direct impact on the organization's bottom line. In the *Harvard Business Review* report *The Impact of Employee Engagement* on Performance, respondents connected high levels of employee engagement to high levels of customer service, productivity, continuous quality improvement, innovation, and strong sales and marketing capabilities.

So, how do companies develop good managers?

Organizations may already have management development programs in place. Yet, such programs typically happen during two distinct timeframes. The first is when employees who have been identified as high potential or high performing participate in programs and then are promoted at a later date. The second is when employees are promoted to management, fail miserably, and then are sent to a management development program.

There's another way to bridge the gap in providing development to a key organizational segment between when employees join management and when they receive development: through new manager orientation.

In this issue of TD at Work, I discuss:
- management orientation and how it differs from other management development programs
- why a manager-specific program is needed
- ways to gain buy-in and support for a manager orientation program
- how to design a successful program using the ADDIE or a similar model
- methods for evaluating your program.

Orientation's Place in Onboarding

Most employees, even if they aren't managers, have been through some type of employee orientation in their careers. This event is a part of the overall onboarding process. Orientation is usually a one-day (or less) event that introduces new hires to the company, its products and services, and the company culture. During orientation, new employees complete any new-hire paperwork and learn the organization's basic code of conduct and important company policies such as anti-harassment and ethics.

In addition to orientation, onboarding commonly includes preboarding, which welcomes candidates after they accept a position and covers first-day logistics. The full onboarding process can take up to a year for new hires to complete because it's about new employees learning their role and becoming productive. It picks up where orientation leaves off and traditionally involves employees' managers, co-workers, and other key stakeholders. It also typically includes on-the-job training, workplace socialization activities, and relationship building.

Organizations consider onboarding essential to employee success. Nearly 98 percent of executives polled in a Korn Ferry FutureStep survey said that onboarding programs are a critical factor in employee retention. After all, companies can't engage employees who don't stay.

Manager-Specific Orientation

How, then, does manager orientation differ from new-hire orientation and other manager development programs? It isn't simply new-hire orientation for a management audience. For example, while both new individual contributors and new-hire managers may get a briefing on the company's history, mission, and vision, new managers will need to understand their critical role in that mission—the bigger picture, the role they have in retaining talent, and so forth. Further, manager orientation is the opportunity to set expectations about what being a manager means. It can serve as a reminder of what it feels like to be in a new role, a feeling that will be helpful for managers as they become responsible for hiring, engaging, and retaining talent.

The real benefit that manager orientation programs provide—beyond setting the stage for a manager's new role—is consistency. A company-wide, consistent definition of management enables organizations to set performance expectations for managers. And managers likewise need to perform consistently. Doing so reduces favoritism and bias when interacting with candidates, employees, and customers and strengthens the company culture. Organizations accomplish their business strategies when employees do the work and perform at a high level—and that happens with good managers.

Manager orientation programs, like manager onboarding, are not replacements for the company's existing management development program. Most of the knowledge and skills that employees learn during a management development program—such as decision making, leadership, and critical thinking—are skills that they can immediately apply on the job. Even if they never become managers, they can use the information they learned from the program.

During the overall manager onboarding process, new managers learn how to interview and conduct performance reviews. They don't need to know those aspects on their first day. However, manager orientation equips new managers with the knowledge and skills they need on day one. The event is designed to complement—not replace— onboarding and management development.

Like any training program, orientation, or onboarding, design is critical for success, as is laying the foundation for the program. Here are steps to take to develop manager orientation.

Step 1: Lay the Groundwork for Manager Orientation

Search for the definition of *management* on the Internet, you'll find that the discipline of management includes five functions: planning, organizing, staffing, leading, and controlling. Management is not leadership. Yet, leading is a part of management.

That is exactly why before you, as the HR or talent development professional, even start developing a manager orientation program, you need to reach consensus within the organization on its definition of and goals for management. That's also why manager orientation programs aren't and shouldn't be considered a duplication of the company's existing leadership development programs. They aren't the same things.

Define Management

Gathering stakeholders in a room and starting a brainstorming session about what management means to the company may be difficult, if not impossible. The most vocal participants will likely dominate the conversation before it dissolves into a fruitless effort. Instead, you may need to think outside the box to reach consensus on a definition for management.

Choose a group of stakeholders ranging from senior leaders to current managers to individual contributors to weigh in on what management means in your organization. Ask each stakeholder to anonymously submit a personal definition of management. You could facilitate this via a platform like SurveyMonkey where the names of individuals are not associated with their responses.

After collecting the responses, do something fun or visual with them, such as running all the text through a word cloud generator. The generator will make the most-often-used words stand out. Bring that word cloud or visual element with you to a meeting with those stakeholders and use it as the starting point of the discussion. Let participants talk about whether all the prominent words should be included or what order the words should be in. Draft several definitions and suggest the group spend some time thinking about them.

Five Functions of Management

If the group responds favorably to the survey activity, repeat it by having participants rate the draft definitions and include an open comment box for additional feedback. It's possible you will receive information that didn't surface during the meeting, either because no one wanted to say it publicly or because the time spent pondering the definitions raised new suggestions.

At this point, you may need to conduct some research. For example, if a commenter mentions that managers are responsible for budgeting, you will want to confirm that the majority of managers participate in the budgeting process.

Reconvene the stakeholders, relay the survey results, refine comments, and together finalize the definition. You will also want to review company job postings, job descriptions, performance reviews, training programs, and related materials to ensure that the new definition of management is clear and consistent in all company communications.

Goals of Management

Once you and the stakeholders have agreed on what managers do, discuss the goal—or desired result—of management. While staffing is something managers do, it's not the goal. The same can be said of controlling, leading, organizing, and planning.

A manager's goal is to hire and train replacements. To accomplish that goal, managers need to perform all the management functions (see the figure).

Managers need to create a plan to achieve their goal. And they must organize the steps necessary to accomplish the plan. Further, managers need to identify the right candidate and provide leadership and support to that individual. Finally, they must regularly evaluate that employee's performance against the established performance standard.

Organizations want managers to understand and embrace the goal of management. Hiring and training their replacement encourages managers to learn and use the art of delegation. Granted, learning how to delegate isn't easy. Being a good delegator involves learning how to relinquish power, control, and authority under the right set of circumstances. But the rewards and opportunities for managers who learn how to delegate can be limitless.

Managers who delegate well are the ones who are invited to work on the CEO's pet project or be a part of the project team tasked with implementing the next big thing for the company. Those work experiences develop managers for future opportunities. Managers' growth and development attained through these projects build the company's talent pipeline and succession plans.

> **A manager's goal is to hire and train replacements.**

If an individual with poor delegation skills is promoted to a management position, chances are he will find himself doing both the new job and the old job at the same time when he should be focused on his new role. He will already be spread too thin—and that doesn't help anyone.

When, with the stakeholders' support, you take the time to define the role and goals of management, then the focus of a manager orientation program will begin to take shape. Now you can identify what existing programs, if any, are in place to help managers learn the management functions so that you do not duplicate these existing programs when you develop the manager orientation program.

Stakeholder Buy-In and Support

Consensus-building activities—such as the survey—not only lead to a definition of management, but they also create organizational buy-in. Every key stakeholder has the opportunity to participate, both anonymously and in person. That type of activity provides you with an opportunity to discuss the management role in an objective way. Begin by giving a report about manager performance, engagement, and retention. Pull this information from the company's learning management system, employee engagement surveys, or exit interviews. Your report doesn't have to be a conversation about a single manager or a single department.

Instead, present a high-level overview of where things are right now and why defining the role of management is in everyone's best interests.

Your report on the current state of management could also serve as a benchmark for comparison later after you've implemented and evaluated the manager orientation program.

Stakeholder buy-in and support are not only critical for developing the manager orientation program but also for sustaining it. Think about what kind of message the company would send if it canceled the program. Take your time and gather the right support. That means not only securing senior management's sponsorship for the program but asking leadership what it takes to retain their support. There's a difference, and it's worth finding out the answer.

Step 2: Design the Manager Orientation Program

If you're familiar with the traditional ADDIE model of instructional design—that is, analysis, design, development, implementation, and evaluation—then you know that step 1 in developing a manager orientation program was the analysis phase. Step 2 is design and development. (Note: I am not advocating that you use the ADDIE model. Use a model you are comfortable with; the process will be similar.)

The good news for designing the manager orientation is that you don't need to start from scratch, even if you are newer to the organization. The program design may overlap with other programs you have designed previously.

First establish the orientation's objectives, which will determine the program's length. Remember, this program should complement existing management L&D activities. It doesn't need to be lengthy but does need to be effective.

Also remember that orientation doesn't have to be a single event. Many organizations don't take advantage of this and try to cram too much into a single session. There's no rule that says orientation must take place all at the same time and all during one day. If you're questioning whether it's best to have one longer session or two shorter ones, talk with your stakeholders. They will tell you what they're prepared to support, and that maintains their buy-in for the program.

The program objectives will give you some sense of what the program will be as well as when it will take place, the timing, and who is responsible for which activities, including whether multiple departments will play a role. For instance, in a typical new-hire orientation, other departments may be involved—such as facilities giving a tour or accounting talking about payroll. Manager orientation may be the same.

Objective 1: Develop Trust

One of your biggest roles in an organization is as a consultant. You offer managers a place to talk about what's happening—both the good and the bad—in their departments. But managers need to trust that the HR or talent development team will provide good advice. New managers may find it difficult to visit you to discuss an employee relations issue if they don't have a relationship with you. Some new managers may feel like they are being judged, even if that isn't the case.

Manager orientation is where you start building trust. Make one program objective to explain what your team does and begin a positive relationship between you and managers.

That doesn't mean creating a slide with a list of the functions you perform and telling managers, "Come to us if you run into any of these situations." Rather, it means taking proactive actions to create trusting, positive relationships with management.

Be Friendly and Approachable

It is possible for you to be nice and enforce company rules at the same time. You can have a cup of coffee or tea with a manager and still talk about company policies. In general, people trust those who are likeable. When designing the management orientation program, build in moments for you and your team to simply chat with new managers.

Keep Confidences

If employees or managers come to you to speak confidentially about an issue or situation, maintain

Management-Focused Activities

These five common activities focus on management functions. Although beyond the scope of orientation, consider them when designing your orientation program, because they will often complement the program you are developing.

Interviews
Organizations may say that some aspects of management, such as proven planning skills, are requirements for securing the job. As such, companies will have several targeted behavioral interview questions to determine how much a candidate knows and has done related to planning. Further, companies may expect internal candidates up for promotions to have worked on their planning skills since they joined the company and will ask a series of questions related to planning during the internal interview.

Management Development Programs
The programs are sometimes referred to as leadership development programs, because through them employees whom companies are developing for roles with greater responsibility will learn leadership. Development programs also often cover topics such as communication skills, problem solving, and decision making. Employees who participate in management or leadership development programs can immediately use the skills they learn. They don't have to wait until they become a manager to apply problem-solving capabilities or demonstrate leadership.

Supervisory Skills Training
Depending on a supervisor's responsibilities, this type of training could happen in a classroom, but it can also happen on the job. The topics that fall under this program are more aligned to specific job responsibilities. For example, a new supervisor who will oversee a team may attend interview skills training so she can staff her department. On the other hand, if a new supervisor will be managing a process, he may attend project management training. At some point, both people and process managers may attend presentation skills training because they have to present reports to senior management.

One-on-One Conversations
Think of these conversations as focused two-way discussions with a structured agenda. One-on-one conversations aren't about one person telling another what to do. They're about two people having a conversation that is usually focused on performance. The discussions could be about what's going well or what needs improvement. Managers and employees should view themselves as both senders and receivers of information during these meetings. These are moments where they are not only communicating the performance standard but providing insights about levels of actual performance.

Model the Rules
The talent development and HR team is often known as the keeper of company rules, policies, procedures, and guidelines. That means you and your team must follow them. Create rules that everyone can easily follow so organizational culture doesn't end up being "Do as I say, not as I do."

their trust and confidence—except when you can't. Be truthful and direct when someone says, "I have something to tell you, but you can't tell anyone." If you can comfortably maintain the individual's confidence, then do so. But when the situation warrants you sharing with appropriate individuals, it's important to your credibility to say so.

Objective 2: Incorporate Adult Learning Principles

Onboarding is about learning; manager orientation is about covering topics that managers need to learn. You can put anything into manager onboarding, but the same is not true for manager orientation. There's a limited amount of time, and your goal should be to optimize it.

Adult learning principles can help you prioritize what makes the most sense for orientation versus the other manager programs the company offers. Note: A full assessment of manager learning and subsequently shifting some content among training and development programs may be warranted. While that will require time and effort, it could ultimately make managers better at their jobs.

Adult learning experiences differ from those we had as children and teens. Adult learning is much more dynamic and centered on participants. Consider these three principles when designing the manager orientation (or any adult learning experience, for that matter).

Deliver the WIIFM (What's in It for Me?)
If you want adult learners to pay attention, tell them from the start why the learning activity is important—not why it's important to the company, but why it's important to the participant. Is it to make their jobs easier, reduce hassles, increase quality, or something else?

Incorporate Real-Life Experiences
Bring real-life experiences into the orientation and ask participants to do the same. That ties back to delivering the WIIFM. As a designer and deliverer of learning experiences, you can't simply promise managers that their job will be easier because of the learning activity. You have to show them through real-life examples and stories. Ask participants to share their stories to further demonstrate how the learning activity will positively affect their work.

Vary Content Delivery Methods
Because it's impractical to design a customized experience for each manager, your goal should be to incorporate various elements—such as opportunities for self-directed learning, collaboration, and feedback—so there is something for everyone. With today's learning technologies, you can spice up learning activities with self-directed exercises, collaborative activities, as well as check-in and feedback sessions.

Objective 3: Determine Relevant Content
Consider the specific topics you should include in the orientation and the overarching message that they should convey. The final list of topics will be contingent on the time allocated for manager orientation, the topics covered in other programs, and the responsibilities that managers have, the latter of which will be contingent on stakeholder or senior leader requirements or feedback.

Also consider the depth to which the orientation will go on each topic. For example, instead of a deep dive on a particular topic, you may opt to only include a

---

ABCD Program Objectives

Program objectives are the expected takeaways from a learning activity and the means for measuring and evaluating the program. The key to writing good program objectives is using the correct verbs. Weak verbs will result in weak metrics, and weak metrics will not properly show the program's value.

The ABCD method is a guide for crafting strong, measurable program objectives:
- audience
- behavior
- condition
- degree

Consider this sample objective: *After attending manager orientation, managers will be able to conduct onboarding for their new employees within a week of the employee's first day.* The audience consists of *managers*. The behavior is *to conduct onboarding*. The condition is *after attending manager orientation*, and the degree is *within a week of the employee's first day*.

This is a specific objective and one an employer can measure. The organization can track the managers who have attended manager orientation. It can also track whether employees received onboarding as well as whether that occurred within employees' first week. Finally, the company could compare the performance of employees who received onboarding within their first week to employees who did not to see whether this is a valuable objective in the manager orientation program.

refresher. Or possibly orientation will provide an introduction to something that another program covers in more depth.

Organizational Aspects

New managers will need to understand the organization's bigger picture, something that they didn't need to as individual contributors.

Vision and mission. Yes, managers are already aware of the company vision, mission, and values. The question now becomes whether they are aware of their new role in helping the organization achieve those. This is where the definition of management comes into the conversation, because a significant part of managers' role is staffing, controlling, leading, organizing, and planning for the employees who will get the work done.

Products and services. New managers may be aware of some aspects of the business, but they will need the big picture, including understanding business trends and financial forecasts. It could be advantageous—depending on your industry, products, and services—to have managers test-drive products or participate in mystery shopping experiences to get the customer point of view. New managers should have access to financial reports and learn how to read them.

Liability. From a legal perspective, managers are often considered agents of the organization, meaning their actions can place the company at legal risk. In some cases, the managers themselves can be personally liable. Give managers the tools to understand legal risk and what to do when they have questions. They don't have to face these challenges alone.

Goal setting and performance measurement. Employees typically work with their manager to set goals. But that process changes when they become managers. Often, managers have to establish their own goals, including how they will obtain the resources (including forecasting and budgeting) to accomplish those goals. This learning may extend beyond orientation, but it is essential to include an introduction to goals and budgets.

People Considerations

Whether people or project managers, individuals new to management have a higher-level role in the organization,

> **The principles of adult learning can help you prioritize what makes the most sense for orientation.**

and that affects their direct reports as well as other employees. Be sure to stress the people side of management during orientation.

Role-modeling company culture. Employees are aware of what the company culture is and whether they can play a part in shaping it. That doesn't change when they become managers. What does change is that they must model company culture, because they hire and evaluate employee performance.

Delivering customer service. New managers need to know the organization's expectations where customer service is concerned. You may want to share the company's Net Promoter Score with managers. Further, you may want to provide managers with training on what they can and can't do to make a customer happy and how to deliver those messages to customers.

Building relationships. Remember that managers hired from outside the company have no established internal relationships, and they will need those to get things done. Similarly, those internally promoted may know other managers, but it's possible that they have not built relationships at that level. This element also ties into managers' relationships with your team.

Using technology. This aspect of orientation isn't specific to a particular software—those discussions may be better for onboarding. Rather, managers need to understand how embracing technology will help them get work done. Equally important is that they understand when not to use technology—for example, during certain employee communications, such as when providing discipline. Sometimes technology can be a manager's best friend, and at other moments, face-to-face communication is necessary.

Mentoring Matters

One of the biggest challenges facing new managers is establishing the right relationship with employees. If the manager is hired from outside the organization, he will need to learn the company and build relationships with new team members. If the new manager is internally promoted, then he has the advantage of knowing the company culture and may even have some established history with employees. But those advantages can also be challenges. Newly promoted managers need to transition from being friends to being friendly. Although possible, that's not easy.

Whether managers come from outside the company or are promoted from within, they can benefit from a mentoring relationship. For instance, mentors can clue new managers into unwritten expectations.

When an individual is hired or promoted to management, you and the hiring manager will talk to the person about the position. That conversation usually aligns with the job description, performance goals, and possibly bonus plans. Yet, new managers often don't hear about the unwritten expectations, such as attending company events or answering emails on weekends. A mentor can help new managers understand those unspoken expectations.

Further, every company has rules and traditions that aren't documented but are company-wide expectations. While these typically aren't negative rules, new managers need to know them. Going to HR or their supervisor could be awkward for new managers, but a mentor could be a confidante and provide some guidance about what's real and not.

Another aspect for which there is no manual is navigating office politics. This isn't backstabbing, career-threatening politics. It could be as simple as understanding what happens at the proverbial "meeting after the meeting." Or when employees try to tell the new manager that this is how things happen around the company, new managers won't have the background and history to guide them. A mentor can show them the ropes and fill them in on this knowledge.

Maintaining manager well-being. Taking on a new role can be stressful, even when individuals are well prepared for it. Managers who show signs of burnout and stress could pass that along to their teams. New managers should be aware that occasional stress is OK but also know how to spot the signs of unhealthy stress. It's possible that providing some learning content in the areas of stress management, time management, and curation could help new managers transition well.

Continuing learning. Manager orientation isn't the end of the learning journey—it's the beginning. Take the time to tell new managers how the company plans to contribute to their success moving forward, such as what happens after orientation. This conversation should include onboarding but possibly management development programs as well as feedback sessions with other members of the management team.

Presentation Considerations

You can cover both the organizational and people-related topics in a variety of ways, including formal classroom discussions, lunch & learn activities, or one-on-one conversations. You can facilitate them face-to-face or online, particularly if the manager has remote responsibilities. This is where your organizational culture can drive who presents the information and how. Have fun with it. Possibly get other managers involved. But always remember the goal: Manager orientation is about setting up new managers for success, because at some point, the organization will want to measure their progress.

Step 3: Implementing and Evaluating the Program

On the surface, it may seem like there isn't much to do when it comes to implementing the manager orientation program. Just roll it out, right? In fact, you have a lot of little details to consider. For example:

- When is the best time to implement the program (time of year, day of the week, and time of the day)?
- Who should be in the first group to attend the program, and what criteria will you use to determine this?
- How will you invite people to participate in the first program (email, LMS notification)?

Further, how will the orientation incorporate current managers who could benefit from the orientation? One option is to consider conducting a pilot group—or possibly two—with current managers.

Importance of Piloting

Pilot groups are the program's dress rehearsals. They enable you to see the activities in action and possibly tweak the program as needed. They give the facilitators an opportunity to work with the content live and get comfortable with it.

Most important, pilot groups are an opportunity for a group of participants to see the draft program before it officially launches. The individuals invited to participate in a pilot should be current employees—in this case, managers. They would attend the program for two purposes:

- **To provide participant feedback.** Current managers can think back on when they became a manager and provide feedback regarding the content's value. It's possible they may make comments such as "I didn't know that" or "I wish I had this type of training when I became a manager." On the other hand, be prepared for managers to say things such as, "I understand that's the policy, but no one does that on the job" or "I've been here seven years and have never used that information." Pilot groups provide a certain level of validation. Hopefully, the feedback doesn't result in a major redesign, but it's better to get that feedback prior to full implementation.
- **To gain their buy-in.** You already secured initial buy-in from stakeholders, but once the program is fully implemented, it's essential to maintain buy-in. New managers must have the time to attend this program. If they are pressured to attend, then you've created a program no one participates in. When the pilot group managers attend the program and think it's fantastic, they will encourage direct reports or other managers to attend. They will mention during interviews that new managers are set up for success starting with manager orientation. They may even mention that they attended one of the pilot sessions and had direct input into the program.

In thinking about pilot group participants, don't shy away from inviting both the program's biggest supporters as well as its harshest critics. It's a good thing to silence the critics. Remember, the goal is to have a valuable manager orientation program. All feedback is welcome and will make the program stronger.

Proving the Management Orientation's Worth

A strong manager orientation program delivers on its promises. It accomplishes its goals and objectives. So, how do you measure its effectiveness?

A common tool for evaluating a training program is Donald Kirkpatrick's levels of evaluation. Reaction (Level 1) is the degree that participants found the program valuable. Learning (Level 2) refers to the extent to which

Measuring Employee Satisfaction

The Net Promoter Score is a measure of a customer's willingness to recommend a company's product or services. Many organizations use it to gauge customer satisfaction and often collect the data via a one-question electronic survey after a customer transaction: "Would you recommend us to your friends and family?"

As you consider ways to measure the manager orientation program's success, you could take the Net Promoter Score further, as some companies do, and ask employees the same question: "Would you recommend this program to other managers?" This is a good indicator of employee satisfaction and a measurement tool at your disposal.

participants acquired the intended knowledge or skills. Behavior (Level 3) is the degree that participants apply what they learned. Results (Level 4) is the extent that the learning affects the organization.

One key aspect of the Kirkpatrick model is the inverse relationship between the data's usefulness and the degree of difficulty in collecting the data. For example, a Level 4 evaluation provides the most valuable data but is most difficult to collect. Meanwhile, Level 1 evaluation data are the easiest to collect but will not provide the same usefulness. That isn't to say that Level 1 evaluations aren't helpful, but they may not be as helpful as a higher-level evaluation.

Decide early in the process how your organization wants to measure program results and what factors to measure. It may be necessary and beneficial to include these as elements in your initial senior management buy-in meeting. You don't want to design and implement a program only to hear that your measurement of success doesn't matter to senior management.

For manager orientation, a Level 1 evaluation is absolutely necessary. It will make new managers—that is, program participants—feel special. There's a big disconnect in messaging when you tell new managers that the company wants to invest in their success, send them to manager orientation, and then neglect to ask for their feedback on the program.

That said, a Level 1 evaluation may not be enough for senior management. Depending on the reasons your company wants the manager orientation program, traditional talent development metrics may be better. Consider these four examples:
- **manager engagement**—more productive managers who are better connected to the company
- **manager performance ratings**—better 90-day or overall performance appraisal ratings
- **manager turnover**—more successful managers who don't want to leave, improving manager retention
- **internal promotions**—a higher number of better candidates for internal job postings, so employees see that the company will give them the tools to be successful as a first-time manager.

Finally, while presenting the numbers is important, there's still value in a good story. Check in with new managers after orientation to make sure their transition to management is going well. You can do this electronically—many onboarding and LMS solutions offer survey capabilities—or in person over coffee or tea. Ask new managers:
- What's been going well so far?
- Has anything not gone as planned? If so, what?
- Which colleagues have been the most helpful?
- How can I help you succeed over the next month?
- What can I do to better prepare future managers?

Implementing and evaluating a new program is tough. Yes, you may be relieved that the program is out of the design phase, but now the real work begins. Monitor feedback from participants, facilitators, and senior management. Everyone needs to see the program's success.

Finally, as the organization grows and changes, make sure the manager orientation program (and other development initiatives) is keeping up with the times. Regularly review the content with key stakeholders to ensure it stays fresh and continues to deliver results.

Conclusion

Today's organizations want to operate with less bureaucracy and more efficiency. They're looking for managers who can delegate and empower employees. That means creating a system of management development that supports managers from day one.

Manager orientation programs aren't stand-alone programs but rather a point in time that brings other programs—like management development and manager onboarding—into alignment. Your goal is to educate new managers about their role and set expectations for the future. The more managers know about being good managers, the better they will staff their departments, lead their teams, plan their strategy, organize the work, and control resources effectively.

References & Resources

Books

Fitz-end, J., and B. Davidson. 2002. *How to Measure Human Resource Management*, 3rd ed. New York, NY: McGraw-Hill.

Haneberg, L. (ed.) 2012. *The ASTD Management Development Handbook: Innovation for Today's Manager*. June. Alexandria, VA: ASTD Press.

TD at Work Issues

Lauby, S. 2018. "A Road Map for Onboarding Managers." *TD at Work*. Alexandria, VA: ATD Press.

Tynan, K. 2017. "Develop Management Skills With the ACCEL Model." *TD at Work*. Alexandria, VA: ATD Press.

Online Resources

Beck, R., and J. Harter. 2015. "Managers Account for 70% of Variance in Employee Engagement." Gallup, April 21. https://news.gallup.com/businessjournal/182792/managers-account-variance-employee-engagement.aspx.

Harvard Business School Publishing. 2013. *The Impact of Employee Engagement on Performance*. https://hbr.org/resources/pdfs/comm/achievers/hbr_achievers_report_sep13.pdf.

Korn Ferry. 2017. "FutureStep Survey: 90% of Executives Say New Hire Retention an Issue." March 21. https://ir.kornferry.com/news-releases/news-release-details/korn-ferry-futurestep-survey-90-percent-executives-say-new-hire.

Lauby, S. 2015. "Your Goals as a Manager: Find Your Replacement," HR Bartender, August 2. www.hrbartender.com/2015/recruiting/your-goal-as-a-manager-find-your-replacement.

———w. 2017. "4 Ways to Measure the Success of Your HR Programs." HR Bartender, January 24. www.hrbartender.com/2017/training/4-ways-measure-success-hr-programs.

Lawson, K. 2017. "Orientation or Onboarding?" *ATD Links*, September 7. www.td.org/newsletters/atd-links/orientation-or-onboarding.

Russell, L. 2009. "The Fundamentals of Adult Learning," *ATD Links*, November 4. www.td.org/newsletters/atd-links/the-fundamentals-of-adult-learning.

Statement of Ownership

TD at Work (Publication number 2373-5570) (Act of August 12, 1970: Section 3685, Title 39 U.S. Code.) Date of filing: September 24, 2019. Frequency of issue: monthly. Annual subscription price: All access: $129; List: $99. Publication and general business offices: 1640 King Street, Alexandria, VA 22314. Editor: Patty Gaul. Known bondholders, mortgagees, and other security holders: none. The purpose, function, and nonprofit status of ASTD DBA Association for Talent Development has not changed during the preceding 12 months. During the preceding 12 months, the average number of copies printed for each issue was 450; the average number of copies distributed, 360; paid electronic copies: 1,023. The figures for September 2019: 450 copies printed, 360 paid distribution, 13 free distribution, 373 total distribution, 1,023 paid electronic copies.

Job Aid

Manager Orientation Program Development Guide

As you approach developing a manager orientation program, keep the project on track and focused using this one-page guide. Based on the ADDIE (analysis, design, development, implementation, evaluation) design model, the guide serves as both a project overview and a tracking tool.

Analysis	**Answer these questions to get started:** • What's the organization's definition of management? • Based on that definition, how are managers doing from a performance perspective? • What programs are currently in place to help managers learn their role? What's missing?
Design	**After the analysis, discuss these details with stakeholders:** • What are the objectives of the manager orientation? • How much time can we dedicate to the program? • Who will own and maintain the program? • What delivery methods will be most effective? Who will be responsible for delivering the content?
Development	**When designing the program, get stakeholder buy-in for these areas:** • What topics should be included in the program? Do we have enough time to cover them? If not, how will new managers learn the rest of the information? • Are there topics we need to include in another program? If so, when will we be able to revise that program? • Who are the subject matter experts for these topics? • Do we have the resources to develop materials in-house?
Implementation	**Before rolling out the new program, consider these options:** • Use pilot groups to secure buy-in and make final content revisions. • Use a phased implementation schedule if resources are limited.
Evaluation	**When deciding how to measure the program, remember:** • Don't create a new metric if an existing one will do. • Ask senior management what they want to see. • Tie results to program objectives. • Anecdotes can be just as valuable as numbers; solicit both qualitative and quantitative data.

Job Aid

Manager Orientation Content Guide

Managers play a key role in an organization, and they need their own orientation program. When designing the program, consider the specific topics to include and the overarching message that they should convey. Use this guide to help you make content decisions, answering the questions and adding relevant notes below each topic area.

Note: The final list of topics you will cover will depend on the time allocated for manager orientation, the topics covered in other programs, and the responsibilities that managers have, the latter of which will be contingent on stakeholder or senior leader requirements or feedback.

Organizational Aspects

New managers need to understand the organization's bigger picture. For those internally promoted, this is something they didn't need to grasp as individual contributors.

❑ **Vision and mission.** For example, how do managers help the organization achieve its vision and mission?

_____

_____

❑ **Products and services.** New managers will need the big picture, including understanding business trends and financial forecasts. What do you need to relay during orientation?

_____

_____

❑ **Liability.** Instill upon new managers that, from a legal perspective, they are often considered agents of the organization, so their actions can place the company at legal risk. What are relevant legal policies or liability risks that managers need to be aware of?

_____

_____

❑ **Goal setting and performance measurement.** Orientation is often a good place and time to introduce new managers to goals and budgets, though both will require more in-depth learning later. What are high-level aspects of these areas that managers need to know on day one?

_____

_____

People Considerations

New managers now have a greater role in the organization than they previously did. Stress the people side of management during orientation. This is applicable to both people managers and project managers.

❑ **Role-modeling company culture.** What are the organization's expectations around how managers model the company culture?

_____

_____

Job Aid

Manager Orientation Content Guide (Cont.)

- **Delivering customer service.** Customer service is everyone's business, but given managers' higher profile, customer service becomes even more important. What customer service skills do you need to remind managers about?

  _____
  _____

- **Building relationships.** Begin establishing trust with new managers and guide them on how to build key relationships within the organization, including with other managers. What steps should they take in their first few days to lay the foundation for good relationships?

  _____
  _____

- **Using technology.** Guide managers on the ways technology can assist them and when to avoid it. How can managers use technology to help them in their daily tasks? When is it preferential for managers to have face-to-face conversations rather than use technology?

  _____
  _____

- **Maintaining manager well-being.** A new role can be stressful. And managers often have their own work while overseeing other employees' work, so their roles can be even more taxing. While some occasional stress is OK, how much is too much? What are the signs of unhealthy stress?

  _____
  _____

- **Continuing learning.** Tell new managers how the company plans to contribute to their success moving forward. What happens after orientation? What other management development programs should new managers participate in?

  _____
  _____

Get Buy-In to Make Change Easier

Read the "Securing Buy-In for Change" digital collection to help you, your organization, and employees work more smoothly through change. Learn how to:

- Solicit answers to employees' comfort level around change.
- Counteract the sabotaging effects of a change process.
- Determine the root cause of change overload.
- Establish whether a potential change-management client is right for your consultancy business.

To learn more, visit:
www.td.org/securing-buy-in